More
Garden
Varieties
Two

More Garden Varieties
Two

AN ANTHOLOGY OF POETRY

With an Introduction
by Patrick Lane

The Mercury Press
(an imprint of Aya Press)
Stratford, Ontario
and *The League of Canadian Poets*
Toronto, Ontario

The publisher gratefully acknowledges the financial assistance of the Canada Council and the Ontario Arts Council.

Production co-ordination: The Blue Pencil

Typeset in Berkeley Old Style and Helvetica by TASK, and printed and bound in Canada

Canadian Cataloguing in Publication:

Main entry under title:

More garden varieties : two

Co-published by the League of Canadian Poets.
ISBN 0-920544-76-2

1. Canadian poetry (English) - 20th century.*
2. Canadian poetry (English) - Competitions.*
I. League of Canadian Poets.

PS8279.M66 1990   C811'.5408   C90-094040-9
PR9195.7.M6 1990

Sales Representation: The Literary Press Group.

The Mercury Press is distributed in Canada by University of Toronto Press, and in the United States by Inland Book Company (selected titles) and Bookslinger.

The Mercury Press
(an imprint of Aya Press)
Box 446
Stratford, Ontario
Canada
N5A 6T3

The League of Canadian Poets
24 Ryerson Avenue
Toronto, Ontario
Canada
M5T 2P3

Contents

INTRODUCTION

I have always been suspicious of contests, particularly when it comes to poetry, or, indeed, any kind of art. Somehow, the idea of artists competing against each other seems to work against the very idea of art and what it means. The impulse to make a poem is a good and wonderful thing and surely that is enough. So when I was asked to be a judge for the League's contest I accepted hesitantly, thinking I was once again working against what I believed was in the interest of poets and poetry. Now that the contest is over and the winners announced I am still not sure if I did the right thing. There were so many good poems. One thousand, six hundred and fifty of them. So many poets.

Yet the poems the other two judges and I chose were remarkable. That it could easily have been three other poems by three other poets is a given. Once the list of poems was reduced to a hundred, and then fifty, the question of which was best was largely academic. Yet the three poems we finally chose seemed to us to stand for everything we thought was best in our poetry in this country.

I think all three judges can say that the individual pieces by Diana Brebner, Blaine Marchand, and D.J. Eastwood are fine, good poems. They are very different from each other in style, tone, and content, yet all three stand together in their expression of what is excellent in writing.

It was a blind contest, as everyone who submitted to it knows. It's strange now to read the list of all the poems that were finally chosen and see the poets' names attached to them. It's strange to realize how different the poems become once I know who wrote them. Many of the names I recognize and so am pleased that they are included, yet during the judging I had no idea who wrote what. Perhaps that is one of the measures of poetry, that the poem itself contains a kind of pristine anonymity separate from the maker. That, I think, is good.

It was, after all, a pleasure to go through the many pages that were submitted to us, to read them both silently and aloud. The final list of the three winners says nothing about all those many writers who submitted work. It does say something about the taste of the judges. Both Miriam Waddington and Joyce Marshall were a pleasure to work with. They were both generous in their desire to find a list of poems that would represent the best of what was offered. I thank them both.

Finally, I would like to say that the winners have written truly fine poems. Their speech, both common and uncommon, holds to that stillness a fine poem must have. I compliment them, am a little envious of them, and wish to say that their particular pieces were the best among the best. Three other judges would have chosen differently, I am sure. But the only three judges this time were us. Next year will be different: the judges, the poets, and the poems. As for my initial suspicions about contests, they have been allayed by the quality of the work that we saw, and the idea that, in the end, what is important is that out there in Canada this past year, one thousand, six hundred and fifty wonderful poems were written. My congratulations once again, to the poets, to my fellow judges, and finally to the poems themselves, those anonymous pieces that here, in this collection, represent the best of who and what we are.

Patrick Lane

DIANA BREBNER

Snow Angels

for John Barton

"in white camouflage like Finnish marksmen"
— Eclogue IV: *To Urania*, Joseph Brodsky

They come across snow, white & camouflaged,
and, from our point of disadvantage,

who can tell what they mean? Or even,
what colour they are, beneath snow

robes, wings, feathers, the primitive
coverings weighing their light bodies down.

Friend, I hope you have seen:
at least one, up close; no more terror

in that than in white marauding bears
with their fanged cavities, black and

blood, red, naturally seeking
you, food, but never victims. Snow angels

come. Across darkness you see them
at their best, holy ghosts of their kind.

Maybe they are as lost as we
can be in snow. Something,

deep and hungry, swallows them.
And in the shaped holes we find: remains,

some celestial parts, and a last message,
desperate, marked in the snow.

BLAINE MARCHAND

The Craving of Knives

The knives are no longer content.
You notice it in the way
the sink their teeth into
lobes of bread,
leave marks as they slice
open the hearts of tomatoes.

For years they seemed so happy,
performing without complaint
the ritual preparation of red meat,
the deboning of fish.
They have allowed
themselves to be pitted against
whetstone by a blunt hand;
they have remained mute,
slotted into racks when no longer needed.
Only recently have they even permitted
their tension
to be taken up
by the grip on their handles.

Such acknowledgement has made them
all the more desperate
to spill out their rich vocabulary
of anger and pain.
Each one wants
to open mouths
along wrists, across necks.

It has led to such rivalry among them.
Only one will be selected
to leave its mark
on the sheets and in the bathtub.
Only one.
And they are frantic,
certain the real intent
will be misunderstood.
The chosen one
picked up,
tagged as merely the weapon.

D.J. EASTWOOD

The Next Stone

my uncle   Samson   he taught me   yep
we we're out in the Gatineaus one day   him and me
I was about twelve   maybe thirteen
and he says   Gerard   Gerard I want you to do something for me
I says   sure uncle   anything
he says   I want you to take this and stay here
while I go stand over there by that pile of rocks

about fifteen paces away there's a mound of smooth round stones
left by a glacier or piled by a settler
before the land went back to bush
that pile I says nodding
that pile says uncle walking over to it

Gerard   he says as he turns to face me
I'm going to pick out about a dozen of these
each about the size of a hamburger   you wait
he digs around in the pile
finds them easily   it's full of saucer size pieces
the kind that would keep you baptizing water with rock
like someone possessed by a stone demon

okay Gerard   says uncle standing straight
I'm going to throw 'em at you
and I want you to shoot them out of the air
no uncle   I says   I couldn't do it
you do it Gerard   and you make sure you aim right
no uncle   I says   I might hit you

my uncle   he doesn't say nothing
just puts them stones down
walks back takes the gun out of my hand says
you go over to the pile Gerard
now
that one word makes me swallow a mouth full of no
I march over to the pile
now   says uncle
you throw them stones at me

I bend
look at uncle standing where I was
the sun in a ball on his head   his back to the hills and bush a
blue sky above the small clearing in the trees
he's looking straight at me
gun hanging from one hand
old beret tucked like a spring leaf
under the brown strap on his shoulder
I know he's waiting
but I don't want to throw
he's my uncle

motionless
I stare into the rolling tree-tipped granite waves beyond him
then he nods
once
I bend   pick up a stone   stand   my hand at my side
he waits again   narrows his eyes
like he thinks I'm not going to throw
I'm just about to say   ready
when uncle says   make damn sure you hit me with that

the cold   in the stone in my hand   entered my bones
a last word fell from his mouth
throw
like a machine for flinging clay pigeons
my arm cocked and released
the stone hurtled towards uncle
his gun came up   pointed directly at me
then my eyes slammed shut and a roar filled my ears
I swear
my heart went deaf and dumb that instant

when my eyes opened
I saw everything
the smiling pile of rocks   the bushes with their green jackets
the blue hat sitting on the heads of the trees
the round ball squinting out of the sky
my uncle with his smooth round stone face
I was alive
but I believe only in death

now
says uncle
throw me the next stone

RAFI AARON

In This Amphitheatre

in this amphitheatre
stones have been a silent spectator
an untransmitting scribe
to our secluded meetings in the night

we sat on stone seats unaware
of Romans and architecture
held our breath to the blackened Judean desert
a poor rival for suspended settlement lights
pinpoints on the frustrated blue skyline

whose conquest over the last streaks of sunlight failed
as the late hour grey
floated unevenly
occasionally to submerge to quiet green

and how i sat alone
when you left me
the vanished desert no longer a mystery
on its empty stage your hair flowed
the settlement lights monopolized the sky
as the need for stars diminished
without your searching hand

to this oasis
i brought you
into my long secluded moments
of marvel at man's hands
embedded perfectly in nature's puzzle
now stained in the fog of your features

i have taken all the symbolism
from these symbols
into which you carved your name
and called night
i cannot erase that enshrined in stone
merely supplement the sullen chapters
with flow of tinted hair

her shivering shoulders from the winter winds
the candle she holds breaks sequence of the stars
and i look onto this night
once again as night

BERT ALMON

The Ancient of Days

College Green, Dublin

On the pavement outside the Bank of Ireland,
a sidewalk artist chalks a picture:
Blake's Ancient of Days, Urizen,
a bearded tyrant leaning from a bright disk
to make order in the void, compasses of light
streaming from his fingers. Windswept clouds
glow a sullen red. College Green has the look
of a world built with compasses: the portico
of the Bank, relentless columns, faces
the blackening walls of Trinity College.

Coins are scattered on the pavement.

Bachelor's Walk, River Liffey

My love of rationality grows
when I look at the white fence that hides
a gutted building: down each narrow board
someone has pencilled thin lines of hatred—

The Jew Bush	electrodes in my
and Israeli CIA	brain to hear
tortured me	everything
I was held in	I say don't
jail for years	think it won't
by the Jew Nazis	won't happen if

There must be a hundred boards inscribed
with this testament, written in public
with a hard pencil. A few raindrops bead
the grainy planks. The graphite is waterproof.

College Green

It's raining hard now, the drawing after Blake
has started to smear. Beside it, a picture
of Donald Duck in a rage, pointing a water hose
at himself, while real water eats away his being.
The coins have been raked up and pocketed.
All through my childhood I laughed at the duck
in the blue sailor suit, all beak and bulging eyes.
Rage was his vocation. He knew his enemies.

GEORGE AMABILE

First Light

One

A washed out morning. Empty
streets, the moth-eaten rug
of dead grass in the park,
the dust, the first
bus bunting its head like a blunt
whale through the quiet...

and over the shadowy hulk
of St. Augustine's church, a full
moon fades like the ghost
of a shocked infant
sucked from the nipple by a storm.

Two

  Though mystery gives way
to belief and belief
  gives way to knowledge
and the small teeth of the mind
  grind on, safety is nothing
but time disguised
  as a clock. Another
day. The air revives
  old failures, old loves
that hover like fragrant shadows
  or cool wings, as we cruise
without too much control
  toward what we're told
are more refined adventures.

Three

In the empty *Safe-*
way parking lot
at the end
of a stormy night

    in a black
    depression
    filled with rain

water, gasoline
refines the drab light
to a garish rainbow—
chartreuse, magenta, peacock blue

    then the painful
    fiesta of dawn
    begins

and suddenly it's clear
that I am a part of the morning
the part that watches
while it burns.

BRIAN BARTLETT

Album

Begin with Great Grandfather's bloody hand
trapped under a cartwheel, his mouth
unhinged in pain, his knees awry.
     Welcome
to my family, to the thronged pages
bearing our invisible thumbprints:

 here, our cat in spasms dropping
 a hairball onto a Persian carpet;
  here, the back of my father's head
  saying what he had to say one day;
here, my mother stooped in the basement
scrubbing our clothes, surrounded
by thick steam, then above a shaggy lawn
a decade of diapers twisting in Fuji blue.

*

 Flip rocks over, the ground
 swarming with signs of the once-lost.

That red-welted, bloated face
was mine, an inexplicable allergy
gripping my eyes half shut. Too young
to be a stoic, holding tales of plagues
at bay, I glimpsed Dad down the hall,
his telephoto lens aimed at my tears.

 Who promised you barbecues, botanical
 gardens, splendid swans with clipped wings?

23

The proud boy's graduation night:
twelve years braking to a halt
with all the parties elsewhere, his tie
coiled at the foot of the bed,
he numbly stretched out shapechanging
the wall, trying not to dream
of snug gowns and perfumed arms.
His feet propped in the foreground
hide half his face from your eyes.

   Who held the camera (if anyone)
   we sometimes can't recall—
   hidden things themselves
   breaking the rocks, blooming unbidden.

In an airport lobby a woman I loved
is holding me, her hair against my neck.
The paper cup crushed in her hand
tells one more story at the end
of many. Two bodies twisting
toward each other from plastic chairs...
   her flight bag on the floor,
     my hands across her back.

  *

   Each of us flinches, each of us
   shakes, falters, our solitude public.
   But these thousand pages also frame

an uncle's miniature coffin
suspended above a pit. Veils, expressionless
lips, hands folded against the cold.

(Mother's brother, uncle
baby, baby uncle, I know nothing
more of you than this: fading sepia
tones, everyone's eyes turned
from your last cradle, you sealed in
at the centre of the picture).

Not to forget Great Aunt Eleanor
spoonfed under a rose-patterned blanket
where Parkinson's disease ruled
her muscles, wrenched her mouth
into a laughless gap.
            See her unposed
clutching onto her elbows for dear life.

*

Don't look away. F4 was the setting
that sluggish December, bouts of rain
near zero, muddy pools multiplying
across the sunken yard. Don't look
away. We all stood angled differently
under hats. Starlings' iridescence
failed to glow, raindrops struck
pools, disappeared. Don't look away.

  Cartwheel, tie, inexplicable allergy.
      From under that rock...
unbidden...

JOHN BARTON

Naked Hearts

Avec un coeur nu dans ton coeur plein,
I will live,
the body's audacity to be learned.

meeting the first evening,
fingers linking somewhere along Saint-Denis.

Shall we stop at Café Nelligan
and drink in the warmth
of candles and mulled wine?

Or shall we walk on

until our eyes meet,
until each insinuation of the flesh

spins us closer,
our gradual skins flowering
with slow desire?

Cross this threshold with me,
discover how deeply the city sleeps.

No one hears us reduce
ourselves to bodies changing
shape in the vivid dark.

The grief of our bodies
retells the world's body of grief.

Draw me between your thighs,
into the search
of mouths, the orifices of love.
Listen to the soft cadences of my sighs.

I had forgotten how my grief
rises, how quickly it wells up
under the tongue's roughness.

Release it, nest in my arms.
Lying here,
the earth is caught in a split-second calm.

I no longer fear to be a man
and we are lovers whether our lovers
are women or men.

Avec un coeur plein dans mon coeur nu,
lie beside me.

In this century those like us
refuse like us
to live as if we have never been.

LAURIE BLOCK

The Fish Plant

forget the head
you can do this with your eyes closed
avoid assholes
riddle of guts
opal eyes
scoop out the heart
think of sex
quick tug in cold blood
here are your tools
flat surface
unforgiving knife
ice

time travels in silver flicks
down the spine
you measure the day
in strips of flesh
until the clock breathes
a bubble empty of fish
an hour of mercy under
the law of the deep
keep your thoughts to yourself
swim for your life

some men angle for pleasure
reel in their deep desires
it's work for you hooked
to an eight-hour day
minimum wage
fish out of water

WILLIAM BONNELL

Bees

That metal extractor--
a big, galvanized drum
mounted on wooden blocks in the basement,
then so tall I had to stand on tiptoe
to peer over the brim.

The combs were trimmed
and shaved with a hot knife,
then slipped inside their wire cages.
You cranked a wooden handle
at first as slow and stiff
as a propeller on some early aircraft
until gradualiy it began to whirr and hum,
rattling at the guy wires
that held it to the floor.

Outside, the steady insect din of summer
had been shut down.
The white hives
were as silent as abandoned hangars,
the remaining bees dormant, wings folded,
fuelled on sweetened water.

That summer was another matter,
busy as pilots on wartime airfields
they'd raided miles for pollen,
thickened combs with honey
and their young,
were merciless on those
they saw as foes.
More than once I watched our neighbour
race in circles around her lawn,
maddening kamikaze crews
tracking relentlessly behind her.

And their hormonal madness
was even worse than ours,
lured out en masse
by their siren queen
they rose and swarmed
to distant trees.
But they were carted
back to barracks
not long after,
their shortlived,
catatonic AWOL no match
against my father's
smoking bark,
his cheesecloth hat
and baggy canvas boiler.

I can still hear it now—
that extractor on an autumn night,
its whirling, heavy thrum,
sucking out the honey
from the combs,
spattering tiny drops
against its walls,
straining to lift off
with its annual cargo.

And bees?
I view them with suspicion,
have, as with all my kind,
the uneasy sense of much unearned.
Dream, at times,
of skies darkened by incessant hordes,
sizzling mobs with debts unclaimed,
those days we'd open hives
and the shrivelled mouse
or mole we'd find
just inches from the door.

LESLEY-ANNE BOURNE

Sweet Sixteen

and I *had* been kissed. And
I was always hungry
but not for sex
which disappointed Ted Filipovich
more than I can say.

There was that dinner he had
his mother's boyfriend (a chef
at Peter's Backyard) set
for my birthday, ready to spring
shut, trap

at the drop of a fork. Teddy,
as captain of the football team,
knew a lot
of cheerleaders we could say, knew
a few things when he requested

pheasant, the wine, all that
chocolate sauce. What could I do
except eat and know
afterwards, on the balcony I would be
too high up, leaning too far out

to say no, after all
he'd waited the whole term
for this, knew, as I said,
how I starved myself,
how good I could be

at it, what my bones
might be hiding— marrow so sweet
he would drink. How could I refuse
a meal like that, another glass,
the sapphire slipped on
my slenderized finger while he whispered,
sappheiros,
making sure that I knew
he spoke other languages,
that the cheerleaders weren't lying.

As he opened his mother's bedroom door
he breathed, *satiate, satisfy,* and
I knew what he wanted to fill.
Anorexia, he whispered as if
this was my name, *such a shame*

to leave these small.

BRIAN BRETT

Deep Inside This Dream

Deep inside this dream
of a white, mechanical tree
standing electric
in a barren landscape,

there's a shadow of human
animals like fleas
moving over the tundra,
looking for a messiah.

Imagine that the polar tree
is the white church of this dream
that will turn it all green again.

Beside the solar
light of the church
is a lake that goes
around in a circle.

Above the lake is a town
and a factory filled
with those dreamers

who dream the old dream
of happy children
sleeping in a jungle,

where all the silver leaves
of the white tree are candy,
and the lake is full of milk
that goes around in a circle.

But the building is made of cement
and the original tree died years ago.
The bellies of the children
are filled with lead and mercury;

a present from the last factory
that went around in a circle
and left the town invested
with interesting diseases.

Yes, the luminous factory pours
its shimmering waste into the circle
of the decaying lake beside
a forest that's already dead.

And under strange coloured lights
the radioactive frogs
glow in the cold night.

JOHN BROOK

This Absence

Today twelve swans flew over
east by north along the Thompson,
pinions pulling the river by.
In their silent passing
— unlike those questing, querulous geese—
absence oppressed me.
It's times like these
you're on my mind:
mornings, I set out
into the unrisen sun,
soap and razor shiny;
much later, the edge taken off me,
I hold the fire-gold sunset
where the river proclaims the lake
and cannot move.

RON CHARACH

Photo

Looking into this picture
 is scanning at high power,
 staring in the mirror too long,
 daring your face to start swimming;
   Yet we keep on staring
though seized by fear
 that one of the soldiers
 might glimpse our hidden hands
 trying to snap this photo—
 (are we a foreign journalist, with immunity,
 or just a Polish workman passing by
 with an okay
 from the soldiers)

A young woman
 her rich black hair piled high
 lies in the street with her lover
 clutching her collar with one hand,
 pulling her lover's head to her own
  with the other
  as though comforting a small child;
  (or the two could be listening
  to a concert in the park)
Her generosity brightens this section
 till it's clear that their slaughter must take place
 in a patch of sunlight.

No rifles have been drawn
 though the soldiers furthest away
 have automatics;
We cannot see what the near officer
 — obviously the commander—
 is stooping to pick up,
 but this action means that the riveting
 is still moments away.

In the foreground,
 the strong back of a second woman
 in an overcoat so light a grey
 that her vertebrae are visible.

Side by side
 are two empty chairs, standing in the rubble,
 and further in the distance, two footstools.
Were they brought in after the softening up,
 for the comfort of the mop-up men?
Or are they merely unkillable things,
 making mockery—

Unmarried men will remember
 the two crouching men (are they brothers?)
 winter hats obscuring their faces
 as they stare into the ground,
 fingers spread out for their captors
 like soft weapons.

But the eye keeps returning
 to our lady of the foreground,
 with her tousled curly hair
 and her broad grey back.
That this hatted, unbowing a people
 could give such voice
 to human hair,
 and at knee-level—

What are these officers fussing with:
Why is one leaning over, reaching for something
 on the other's back?
 more ammunition? a reprieve?
What is on the mind of the corporal
 looking straight on,
 the one most likely
 to spot a gleam from the eye
 of our camera—

Nine professionals, obeying orders,
 in differing states of alertness
 (one whose head is not shown,
 — abstaining)
Five still breathing partisans
 in the rubble of a great city, Warsaw,
 (might one of them not belong here,
 perhaps a sympathizer, caught up
 in history?)

The tense, posturing bodies
 of those about to receive
 form a fault-line through the photo,
 with the beautifully awaiting women
 and their men
 at the centre.

KAREN CONNELLY

Amaya, in Spring

Amaya has come home, though that word is not quite right.
She has returned with chips of winter stuck in her teeth,
                    but it is spring now.
The air is smooth as the flesh over a man's ribs.
Just touching grass, just treading quietly
is almost as easy and far gentler than making love.
The wind breathes Africa on us and the sea
is a sweet juice squeezed up over the sand.
Azkorri's children go to the cliffs and lean back
        into the wind, praying to rise like kites.

In the tradition of the new season, Amaya,
        (my drug addict, my broken poem, my breaker of mirrors)
                is pregnant.

A memory laps on one of my messier shores.
My mother drowns quietly in the slough
of my dead sister's clothes, clutching a thin rope of gold,
        coughing. "But she was so beautiful,"

        as if that was enough
        as if that was anything at all.

Yet that is what I think myself when I hear Amaya
in my bathroom, shaken like a rug by her belly,
rippling again and again over the toilet,
I whisper to the walls, "God, she is so beautiful,"
        knowing this is neither an excuse nor a prayer.

For a month, she scratches about for a willing doctor
        in this Catholic maze of stone houses,
        this village whipped to chastity by winter sleet.
The only abortionist is the greedy surgeon
        (forensic) who spends Sundays
        drinking with her stepfather (policeman).
He calls her a whore.
A trip to France is the only path
        out of the warming hell of her body.

The year does not matter, nor the country, nor season.
And beauty is a talisman in dead myths.
It does not guide her now, beyond the border,
        where she slips blindly on oiled French words.
She dreams awake of the instruments, the keen silver edges.
Any woman dreams of this, in any year season country
but the irony of spring amuses Amaya.

She comes back with a white grin, lips like tight scars.
A fever of infection reddens her,
but she is as blessedly hollow
as the carved dome of a cathedral.
She makes a bed on my floor and sleeps for two days.

Her body remains what it was when I first found her,
slightly thicker than her skeleton,
        a famine's dog, scarcely worth feeding—

        she picks, sucks at eggs, milk,
        glasses of juice, grimaces, still frightened
                by raw vegetables.

She almost remained pure this winter
        shuddering off heroin like a snake
        shedding dead skin,

but her tongue, the corners of her eyes
(unique hiding places for needle-marks)
are still a painter's rags used for the red oils.

When I watch Amaya's face, I glimpse
another lost skin, hear an old voice saying
the same words in a language she does not know.
From deeper shadows, my sister once said,
It is easier to be a memory that it is to be alive.

Amaya? Amaya? She lied.
See yourself, the dark length of hair
        falling down the ravine of your back,
        the bones pearled in pale velvet, the raven-eyes.

Amaya, I whisper, go gently.
A talent for sorrow is almost a talent for love.
Only the key is different.
Sing until you find the other sound.

I speak to the night while she sleeps by my bed.
She rolls over, one white hand hooked like a cloud
between the ridge of her hips and ribs.
Amaya lies dreaming on the floor
caught tight in her own bones.

MARLENE COOKSHAW

I Keep Taking

At a certain point in the universe longing condenses
— Roo Borson

I keep taking my life in hand, over
and over, and setting it down again
like a bargain I cannot afford.

Uptown, the women in rubber band skirts
tell me nothing has changed since
lions and Christians. When I ask
what they mean, they say
something about spectacles and desire.

What is this desire of mine
for new structure, this attempt
to reorganize pieces, to make them speak
some sense?

I want to grow a greenhouse,
enough to feed us all through winter.
I want an In and Out basket.
I want the broccoli never to yellow
in the fridge, I want my favourite
black jeans to recover their seams.

I want two mornings a day.

I want home made soup in the slow cooker,
bread in the oven, peaches
ripe at all seasons. I want
my 13-year-old dog to live another five years,
and five after that.

MARLENE COOKSHAW

I want the canary, when he dies, to float
from the perch in his sleep, head under his wing,
like a dandelion blown before the colour's gone.

I want the strawberries to send runners
to the empty spot.

I want stucco to metamorphose into brick
and this house to grow another storey.
I want my bed on the second floor. I want
nothing to match and everything to speak
its history. I want a salt wind
to parch the rivers in my head
and spring rain to startle the prairie wheat.

I want storms we know the end of.

I want swallows to nest beneath the eaves
and friends to visit for a season.
Private cars dismantled and hammered
into ploughshares, and fluorescent lighting
to cease like a bad dream.
I want the morning silence unsettled
by the neighbour singing laundry on her line,
by the rattle of starlings
beneath her loose shingle,
by the shriek of the early train.

I want me to speak softly and women
to walk with their heels on the ground.

I want to uninvent
perfectly interchangeable parts
— Eli Whitney, do you hear me?
I want the United States to become untied,
I want butter to stop sailing
across the ocean to a country full of cows.

MARLENE COOKSHAW

We must cease taking lives in our hands,
over and over, and setting them down
like a bargain we cannot afford.

We must pull our morning glory by hand
and raise chickens to eat the earwigs.

We must take our own bags to market,
have our shoes resoled and our animals neutered.

We must not scoop dolphins from the sea
as if they were mould on a windowpane, not
cut loose our invisible nets, not cloud
the blue world with tampon applicators.

We must begin to point a finger at ourselves,
to organize the pieces, to make them speak sense.

We must allow what indicates the world
to enter us.

AFUA COOPER

To Khetiwe

So sista
you ask me
what can a woman who likes being big
a woman who enjoys her size
do when other sistas make unfavourable comments about
it and coyly suggest with-loss clinic
"it's not easy being a fat Black woman," you say

I can make a few suggestions
potential replies to throw back at these mahgah women
first tell them that you are into yourself
and because you are into yourself
you're not a slave to fashion
not a slave of babylon
then tell them that thin
might be in
but fat is no sin
next, ask if they know of their ancient traditions
that in southeastern Nigeria
the rich and not so rich used to send their daughters
to Old Calabar to make them beautiful

beautiful in this case meant
fat
      plump
above size 12

MICHAEL CRUMMEY

Small Animals

Little traffic between Sharbot Lake
and Kingston late night Sunday,
the quiet highway does its best
to keep me awake—
        road signs flare up
like tall matches
      speed limits   official
proclamations on litter and populations,
sudden moments of colour
I no longer try to read
        or comprehend.

The car's rumble is a low noise
I make in the back of my throat.

      The eyes of small animals
spark red along the roadside
and go out in the darkness.

We drive through entire towns
asleep and unaware of us,
        only the occasional gold tooth
of a porch light
waiting up for someone arriving late.

And Sarah's sleeping too beside me,
her head against the darkness
of the window.

BARRY DEMPSTER

Adam and Innocence

In the beginning Adam was naive.
Playing names, fussing with
the breeze, pretending to be
a lion or a rock. Whatever
pleased. For God's keen eye
he hung from lower branches
in the shape and dangle of a fruit.
Posed naked on a cliff, a model
moon. The first experiment:
will he devise a language, be
seasonal, will he sink or swim?
Give of himself for the sake of
loneliness? He sat on the cold
hard ground and listened to
the sounds of everything. When
he spoke to streams, he believed
in their memory. Darkness
nothing more than a concealed face.

It is important for children
to learn to eat with forks, to
know that life is round, no Santa
Claus, the body covered up. I teach
little Adam he is neither an orange
nor Spiderman. Do not speak
to strangers, beware of promises.
A night-light glows in the nursery,
a plastic angel with a pink face.

Adam is always an innocent.
In the beginning children are never
reflections of ourselves. Wish
on a newborn, wish for a keen future.
Rather than die, wouldn't we all
choose to be rocks? Or moon about
the universe, like a bunch of angels
warming themselves on children's eyes.
To watch is a lonely occupation:
the inside wanting out. Adam and I
sit on the bedroom floor and I hear
every single sound he makes. I am
swayed by promises of memory. The
simple face beaming through
the shadows of my disbelief.

DEBBIE FERSHT

Akrasia

The Greeks actually had a name for it
that unexplainable pull towards the most
alluring object of desire.

When I was six we had just moved
to Canada from England it was then
I got to meet my aunt Hilda
she took me to a toy store the biggest
I'd seen in the whole world she
told me to pick out one thing anything
I wanted it didn't matter how much
it cost I could have just one thing.

Wide-eyed I wandered the aisles were endless
the shelves stacked sky-high for the first time
I could get anything I wanted this kind lady
this fat lady with the funny accent was giving me
a child's dream.

I couldn't decide I didn't know which was better
a talking Dick Van Dyke or a Barbie doll with
ten different outfits I couldn't make up my mind
how could I just one thing I asked just one she said
and I hated her I hated her how she was making me suffer.

The Greeks called it Akrasia they tried to rid it
through reason but I was only a child, a child
could my aunt not see?

I went home with a Slinky its silvery spine
still needs one simple shove
to get it going.

ERIC FOLSOM

The Woman with Minoan Eyes

learned just as you and I
how to live as poet/derelict/free spirit
the alcoholic in the mirror looking back
move the phone to the dining room table
have another cigar don't let up
you have a week to live
in the famous alley of ashcans
with the dustbin bohemians and the worn
lyrical anarchists, vegetarian dopers
journals, spiral notebooks, meticulously
collected over five years then thrown
like angel wings from a subway platform
we write crude verse, oh children
if these pressed and dried sentiments
should ever reach you, remember...
it was to be a writer
somewhere to go, something to do
buried deep in delusions
be a writer, recording these times
a writer with unique and terrible visions
of the wheel that isn't round
of the damaged fire burning hot
bulging embolism and the doomed
flight of metal fatigue
a voyage to the new world
only to pour wind on the sounds
to pour words on the end of it all
words that themselves will be destroyed
forgotten in the brainscan linguistic
hemorrhage Sappho's fragments in the milk
of skies all the information that
binds paper together slips through
our fingers like neutron stars dissolving
all notions of place until
one person becomes like a rock is
to another rock

NEILE GRAHAM

Storyteller Talking at the End of Her Days

So what is paradise, since we yearn
for it so unevenly and think we touch
it but so fleetingly it is brief as the touch
of the dream's finger to our lips as we sleep

When you read my words to me they escape me.
Paradise seems like hell to me, all that lying
in the sun and sweating lazy sex.
I like mine in a colder climate where
the only warmth is what we ourselves
can generate between us and call passion: the heat
of our bodies coming alive between us.
I know I wander somewhat when I speak; it's because
my mind entertains so many guests— each thought
reminds me of another and they all crowd
in at once too quickly to separate so I embrace
them all. Sure I've travelled had lovers
married had a child and dreams
wrote some of them down. Sometimes I got lost
in the intricate tangle that locked me to a place a time
and I wrote it down, broke away to follow
another thread of the web. A myriad of voices
woven with my own, singing a madrigal
of light, each note a point in the woven sky.
One of my favourite memories is the most simple—
sitting at night on the chesterfield, the rest
of the house asleep, the cat beside me. I
touched her face as though it were mine.
There isn't much I would do again
if I could, you see I haven't yet let go
of it all in my mind. I can unlock it at will
but it all floods in, more than I can control.
I always used to like the feeling of having
more in my hands than I could control.
I used to like dangerous men but I knew
enough not to live with them. I won't tell

you the names of any of my famous lovers;
there's no point, the ordinary was the best,
when the spark of feeling between us wasn't
just pride, and we weren't afraid to let
ourselves be taken... enough of the flesh
for now it weighs me down.
I feel I haven't lived enough have lived
too much have lived on fire trying to dance
so fast the flames would not burn. And now
I'm lying in a snow field flush with the
earth; it's cold but I can see the tangle
of stars in the sky and a few are falling.
Yes it's true, each one is a small ball
of fire like the sun but a few are falling.

Washing at Sunset

My hands touch the water and I'm
crying. Simple as that.
I keep trying to put things together,
more than tears and water
while the sun squeezed
between cloud and mountain

focuses warm as a hand on my back.
I don't move. Wondering why the sky
opened like that, I see
myself in the water
with the sun behind and the dark
shape of the water nodding.

Nodding as if to tell me yes,
say yes to the man in the doorway
who has asked me to stay.
I want to complain that it's not
that simple, nothing is.
It's all too tangled

in years and the ways my body
knows his and knows nothing at all.
And it's this that I fear--the sun
setting over the mountain
like his mouth on my breast
and me wanting to push it

away, to run out into the street
naked, laughing.
It's too late to tell him lies.
The sun on my shoulder
is his hand and our motives are certain:
the parody of self

that is sometimes beauty.
The warm flesh. The fear
I want to name love.
I'm afraid I fall through life
and learn nothing--it is simple as that.
If I could just put it together,

it would all make sense. The sun would
release my shoulder, I'd lift
my hands from the water and throw open every door,
let his skin warm my hands, become
something to hold.
Then say simply yes.

JEFF GRIESBACH

Untitled

You were strong,
with your jug-ears and little black moustache,
sometimes so strong it scared me.
Once I reached back to cast
and snagged my hook in your lip.
You never said a word,
just sat there with the barb
sticking out of your moustache,
blood running down your chin.

I thought of that when I saw you in the hospital,
the cancer eating away at you
inch by inch.
The night before, my mother and aunt
had bought black dresses.
You just laughed,
called me a Dutchman,
twisted my nose and asked if I'd forgotten
where the barbershop is.

You used to laugh like falling mountains,
now it's a raspy wheeze.
You used to chop down trees with an axe
just to show you could,
now you puff using a chain saw.
You tease your grandchildren harder than ever,
but your forehead wrinkles if we tease back.

JEFF GRIESBACH

I never saw them take out the fishhook
and sometimes I wonder if it's still inside you.
Floating through your bloodstream,
it gets bigger and bigger,
tearing kidneys, ripping lungs,
slashing your stomach lining.
The yell you should have given so many years ago
gets bigger and bigger,
explodes inside you.
Rusty fishhooks spray all over the room.

MARGARET HAMMER

Highrise Mondrian

Squares of Caribbean colour
balance in the dark
apartment block
like sharp notes sounded
in an hour of silence.

Dancers jerk and writhe
in the yellow box.
A stoop-shouldered housewife,
against green,
dries the final dish.
Bathrobed, two forgetful figures
crisscross the cerise.

In the orange square
a black cutout
leans, statue-still,
against the window frame.

Suddenly he lifts
a trumpet to his lips,
turns straight toward me
and blows one high, clear note
against the grey walls
of my cell.

LALA HEINE-KOEHN

Will Time Get Better

Time has a bellyache from the hours he cannot digest
he complains, his bowels are gyrating as if break dancing.
Remembering remedies from home, when I was little,
I gave him a spoonful of coal with a glass
 of camomile tea. He retched, the black powder covering
his face and my pink satin quilt he was sitting on.
Recalling still another remedy from the washerwoman
I brewed a tea of ground mare's leaves, gentian and snakeroot.
Adding a pinch of lupulin, I laced it with melted lard
from a she-goat, killed, because her teats dried out like gourds.
He gulped it down and keeled over at my feet.

Now, he is leaning on my shoulders, his arms wrapped
around my neck and I walk him to the cellar, the attic
up and down the stairs to keep him awake. It must have been
the lupulin that made him drowsy, unable to stand on his own.
I keep the conversation going, telling him about the winter
in Poland, the year before last, the heavy frost
and snowfall they had with no wood or coal. And the spring
before, their soil soaked with red rain for the next 30 years.
I flick off dead flies from pictures and windowpanes
as we pass them on the stairs, ask him to repeat:
Chernobyl, Chernobyl to exercise his thick tongue.

Who cares what goes on in Poland or will go on
for the next 30 or 30,000 years. What are years to him?
he babbles, his face distorted with cramps.
Something's always wrong with that hemophiliac country,
it bleeds and bleeds regardless of the weather.
He had his fill of the stories I had brought back
from there this past year. The queues, waiting like hungry snakes
in front of butcher shops, fruit and vegetable stands; the murky
coffee and cocoa ersatz, the grey sugar, the muddy soap.

People on the streets with strings of toilet paper on their necks
counting the precious rolls as if they were Rosary Beads.
No napkins for babies, women using rags...
Bloated more than ever, he clutches his belly, says,
it must have been I who had deceived him, feeding him
all those cuckooflowers, bison grass and mushrooms I had
brought back from there, saturating his guts with that red rain
I was telling him about. And what about the remedies I gave him?
What coal did I use? Was the goat killed because she had
no milk or did the fodder poison her?

My feet are getting tired from walking him up
and down the stairs. In the back of my mind
this nagging feeling: how long will I have to look
after him? Will he ever get better?
If only I could prop him against the wall, to take off
my shoes to change into my new pink slippers I just finished
embroidering...
It's odd— that I can't even remember if I told him about
the little old lady in Warsaw who stood by the kiosk
with its carrots and onions counting her money, then
crossing the street, she bought two bunches of purple
everlasting asters.

LYNN HENRY

Oh

for a moment i forgot
what a soup can is
and a Heinz ketchup label
and Robertson Davies'
beard. For a minute i recalled
my sister in the garden
with a blue trike wheel that
rusted and collapsed. Then
the grass crawled and shivered
the instant that i wondered
why i know all this
and do not know
what crawls in my bones
exactly
like the grass.

KEN HILLS

Summer Signs

I know it's summer

when fat birds tug at slippery worms after a warm rain,
and Mrs. Mason shoos curious dogs from her manicured lawn,
when young ballplayers crowd the playing fields
and proud parents, dressed for the season,
he, with his fat belly, winter's reservoir,
she, with painted fingers and toes and summer tan,
start sentences off with phrases like, "when I was his age,"

when the sun rises before I do
and airplanes from a nearby airport
interrupt long awaited conversations
with a seldom seen neighbour,

when the lake is dotted with white billowy sails
and modern Ahabs, with radio transmitters and sonar devices,
crisscross the choppy Lake Ontario waters
in search of the great lost salmon.

Summer is the season of the mirage,
when, coaxed on by endless sunlit days,
I feel I will live forever,
but, just when I get to feel this way,
the first maple leaf,
the harbinger of summer sleep,
wafts casually earthward
and neighbourhood children clamber on to roadways
for the first road hockey game of the new season.

ALISON HOPWOOD

Debts & Divisions

One

When he remarked that no stranger should spoil the party,
Mirza Ghalib was shown out. What did he expect? He was a poet.

The flute curls out Vivaldi's melody. Violin, cello,
harpsichord sing the same tune. Afterwards the players separate.

Oppressed, the poet makes poetry out of oppression.
Free, the poet may choose the world's woes/dejection/neglect.

Sunflower seeds in the bird-feeder bring chickadees
not crows. In the house, guests are coming for dinner.

"It takes two to make a quarrel" is the saying.
Can one make a friendship?

Two

Burning Rushdie's novel won't ensure the triumph of Islam,
nor our reading him hasten its end.

Pigeon is to falcon, gazelle to cheetah,
as I to you? as you to me? as we are to…

In the story of Philomela and Procne, both suffered.
Which one had her tongue torn out?

Headline: "Teen-age prostitute murdered in alley."
Now she can't tell you about her life.

At the grand entrance to an art gallery said to be "rich
in depictions of the crucifixion," a woman slaps her crying child.

Three

"The cabbage moth looks innocent on the green leaf,"
writes Phyllis Webb. And a smiling face at the door.

The robin is pulling a worm from the ground.
That's the nature of the robin— it has to find a worm.

O here's Marcia— she's invited herself for tea.
The cuckoo, too, goes visiting, leaving its eggs in others' nests.

Pleased, a lover says ~"I love you."
It's not a promise to please the other.

Lines of longitude meet at the frozen pole.
Each on their own path, they march straight to collision.

Four

We all initial these articles: sky is blue, leaves are green.
What else can we put in life's agreement?

A liberated woman rejects her husband's name, takes back
her own name— her mother's husband's name.

"Cree, like most Indian languages, has no gender,"
says Tom Highway, writing of a female Nanabush.

"I can't use this language. It was made by men,"
a certain feminist tells me— cat got your tongue?

"We don't take that play money here," said the Blaine store-keeper
tossing back a green queen, a golden loon dollar.

Five

Saplings and milkweed— "obsolete Nature" says Adrienne Rich,
feeling the cold wind blow between past and to come.

How tall we are— up on the shoulders of the past.
Tomorrow will soon hoist itself on our backs.

"Come, you guys," the mother calls her daughters.
She hasn't heard of Guy Fawkes' gunpowder treason and plot.

This is the "post-modern" age, they say.
Only the old-fashioned are "modern" now.

"Milton! Thou shouldst be living at this hour."
Can you imagine the welcome we'd give him?

Six

Maple leaves and beavers were appropriate, they felt,
to the Songs of the Great Dominion. We smile knowingly.

A mosaic: a pattern formed with bits of stone or glass,
without blending. Does that make a national identity?

To take Troy, Ulysses put the Greeks in a wooden horse.
Here planes arrive bringing investors.

Years ago burning a blanket for potlatching was illegal.
Now, houses are torn down to make room for more pretentious ones.

Our government doesn't oblige immigrants to learn a new language—
not English or French, Inuktitut or Cree— Jehovah's strategy at Babel.

Seven

Ghalib— so foreign, long dead, writing in Urdu—
now in translation offers a pattern to poets,

and Phyllis, high over-head, calls us to follow,
to climb, too, into the twisting Tower,

and Adrienne also tells in her own way
of the pain and the love of her time and her place.

The ways to write poems— the ways to be right
the ways to be wrong— are endless.

Brilliant red and yellow, a giant butterfly goes into the blue sky—
a four-finned kite struggling against its string.

BILL HOWELL

Aya

Pakak Innuksuk is about to sing
about two brothers trapped on the ice.

Pakak Innuksuk grins at his small son
and tells us the missionaries lived so far
away from his village on Baffin Island
the songs were never completely silenced.

Pakak Innuksuk's song has no words
we have ever heard before, yet all of us
have always known this could happen.

Pakak Innuksuk passes his drum
down to his son, and together they sing
quietly about the two brothers
and how the Moon spoke to them.

Dance together as brothers, says
the Moon, *alone in my light until
the Sun finds its lost home
somewhere in your hearts…*

HELEN HUMPHREYS

Nuns Looking Anxious, Listening to Radios

In the picture
three nuns.
Faces slightly upturned.
One holds a radio.
All are smiling.

Perhaps they are listening
to the Papal broadcast.
Or their favourite rock station.
Perhaps they have just
turned the radio off
and this is why they are smiling.

The caption on the picture says:
"Nuns looking anxious, listening to radios."
Well.
There is only one radio.
And they are smiling.
They really are smiling.

Perhaps the person who wrote that
hated nuns. Or gave up religion
because it wasn't any fun.
Because it didn't make them smile.
Ever.

Because of the person who wrote that
the picture isn't about three
smiling nuns with a radio.
It is about the writer's
inability to count.
It is about the writer
as a nun.
It is about the writer.
Only.

LYDIA KWA

First Lessons

In secondary three, Mr. Lam,
our biology teacher—
dwarf with hairy nostrils and
a greased wave of hair perched
like a rooster's comb—
said: *the heart is*
the size of a fist, and puts
his hand to his chest as if in
a war salute

I was taught that biology is
destiny: we are
forever children
of our parents, and girls
must bleed into
women

You have a heart of stone
my papa said, because
I did not speak
to him for months except
hello
when he returned from work
in the evenings

The doctor asked me
to let myself feel
so I said *he beat me*

His fist
ramming the backbone
until my heart gives in
first turning soft
then gradually
hardening.

VIVIAN LEWIN

Into New Country

How could the settlers know
whether the land was fair?
New France was deep with snow
in 1608. Quebec's no
fresh young thing whose mother
phoned her daily. Even the snow
stopped. It got too cold to snow
and the great river froze up
completely. They didn't drive up
from Detroit in summer looking for snow,
their skis on the roof. No, *mon pays*,
your fosterlings had to pay

to be seasick en route, or pay
their passage by wading in snow
so thick *ce n'est pas un pays*,
c'est l'hiver, a winter I pay
for in installments while my fair
French improves a bit: *La paix
du seigneur* I reply and pay
for a candle or some other
token at Notre Dame, the mother
church. Am I a fool to pay
for peace, while further up
north the sky is lighting up

with rippling colour and up-
setting the network show they pay
so dearly for— buy dishes to pick up
American English— filling up
their TV screens with snow
and static? And the wind is up.
Yes, I've done it, pulled up

anchor and cried my last fare-
wells to shore, all in a fair
attempt to get myself up-
rooted and moved to some other
geography. As if home, other

than the planet we call Mother
Earth, were something to add up
or divide, while we mouth our
sincerest allegiance in a mother
tongue we've just learned to pay
our respects in, then mother
still-newer immigrants whose mother
learns French from the sports page, no
small accomplishment. It's the snow
and slippery ice this grandmother
fears. Her footing is only fair.
She thinks it isn't fair

to give up fluency *and* fair
weather. She grumbles, grandmother
does. Unfair. Unfair.
She'll pack her bags. Fare-
well. Off to Florida. Or make up
with us again, iron more fair
linen or knit and lend me bus fare
when I'm limping towards pay-
day or giving classes with pay
to the quilters at the *cercle fer-
mier* who know how well snow
kept the children warm, comforters no

habitante ever stitched piled snow-
white on their houses: the fair
flat attic light of mother-
love both lost and (Elizabeth Bishop
knew it) impossible to repay.

LAURA LUSH

Mr. Ishigami

I have my Japanese lover— almost.
And what sounds will come clear,
the bright blue fields at night
racing like bamboo?
And when he goes to Taiwan
maybe he'll have a girl,
drink in a bar where the window
wears a stirrup of moths.
Or maybe he'll grow a moustache,
give ash to his oak-plane face.
Alone, in the ryokan,
what will he say to me,
now that I sit just like him,
legs crossed, the contentment of frogs
all over my face?
What will he do when I follow the
string of chocolate under his
eyes, pull it back through my mouth,
tongue happier than cherries.

The Worm Girl

I am the Worm Girl.
I drive a Wonderbread truck,
converted— good tires,
bumpers black as jujubes.
Every weekend I drive the Grey Bruce country,
all the silvered lakes,
birches waving like old drunks.

In the back, I have 25,000 worms,
deep in the earth
hidden like coins in a chocolate cake.
Sometimes they wriggle to the top,
luminous as moons,
their skin onion-blue.
What they feel is my hands,
each finger a lure,
urging them out,
gently, like a carrot's mid-wife.
I reward them with light.
They give me warmth,
like a glove of sun.

Sighting the Monks

We walk through the vast palms,
the headless Buddhas,
stone-brown trees.

Nearby, the monks sip on Sprites,
grin their smooth riverbed smiles.
No one heckles them,
asks them to buy postcards,
fans that twist into geese.
They sit, their robes softening
like butter.

We could stare at them all day,
their sandalled feet.
How almost no sound comes from
their bodies, yet eyes that
can disturb whole mountains.

KATHY MAC

Artifacts

We set aside Saturday morning for crowbars
in the basement; peeling back linoleum strata
with as little care as bulldozers at a construction site
chancing across remnants of former inhabitants
                                    a photograph
oval, unfaded, torn in the upper right corner
when my crowbar found it, nailed face down
under its own little bit of floor
                          a face, grey eyes
in the light, taking and not giving,
cheeks and brows haughty and a chin
receding into the starched collar,
black tie tacked into place with an
anchor clasp
                  the only way in, that anchor
the only clue to the riddles he posed
                                    who?
and why so deliberately hidden so long?

On the back in a careless hand
Mr. Conrad 1906

*

Remember our first night here?

opening the fireplace
to find a book— *Victorian Love Poems*—
left on the grate for kindling

---

*

Donna Ree, bella Donna Ree, poison, ill
luck the worst a boat can have
                              broken up
anonymous ribs on a rocky shore
but for her name board, crudely lettered
black on a white ground, the "e"s in
Ree almost running
                    over the border; were
they drunk, who painted her, or is it the end
of long labour? The characters are straight enough,
pride and certainty in their
execution
            not perfection, not
in a boat broken up, one plank only
worth salvage; folk art for some lucky
beachcombers
                    you and I

*

My grandparents left jewelry which
will never really be mine, so I selectively
exercise the right to be generous—pearl
earrings to one sister-in-law, pearl brooch
to another. The rest in a safety deposit box,
amethyst tie clasps, huge rings to encompass
a fisherman's fingers

One signet in particular
not as large as the rest; its message
lost—worn smooth and long since
forgotten
            clean for a new beginning
                              yours
since last Christmas, with love
too thin to re-etch

---

*

Oval portrait of a nameless
great aunt on my mother's side
                    Ariel 1911
the inscription reads and I
believe it; she's as trapped, as lost
as Mr. Conrad between layers
so I framed them both and they hang
on either side of the kitchen mantel
where Donna Ree rested
                            till last Christmas when
I gave you grandfather's ring and
                        the Donna Ree came
crashing down
                dislodged from the place
where it had rested so long
                            a fog of dust
billowed on unfamiliar currents
                            disrupting
our spirits

CAROL MALYON

Old Woman's Pantoum

All these faces are strange
I don't know them
This hallway is empty
It goes nowhere

I don't know them
This woman is a stranger
It goes nowhere
She calls me by my first name

This woman is a stranger
I never answer
She calls me by my first name
I wish she'd go away

I never answer
I want her to call me Mrs. Johnson
I wish she'd go away
Mrs. Johnson, that's my name

I want her to call me Mrs. Johnson
When I tell her, she just laughs
Mrs. Johnson, that's my name
I don't have any decent shoes

When I tell her, she just laughs
I wear old slippers
I don't have any decent shoes
I shuffle like everyone

I wear old slippers
I can't find my glasses
I shuffle like everyone
I need my teeth

I can't find my glasses
A stranger feeds me
I need my teeth
I hate the food so I don't eat it

A stranger feeds me
A stranger pulls my mouth open
I hate the food so I don't eat it
A stranger pushes a spoon inside

A stranger pulls my mouth open
I spit the food out
A stranger pushes a spoon inside
Someone slaps me

I spit the food out
They give me pills
Someone slaps me
I hide pills underneath my tongue

They give me pills
A woman is always in the bathroom
I hide pills underneath my tongue
I watch her spit pills out

A woman is always in the bathroom
We never speak
I watch her spit pills out
When I smile, she smiles at me

We never speak
When I wave, she waves back
When I smile, she smiles at me
The woman in the bathroom is the only friend I have

When I wave, she waves back
All these faces are strange
The woman in the bathroom is the only friend I have
This hallway is empty

BLAINE MARCHAND

First Taste

This was my first taste of it:
age four or five,
up there, in the newsreel
on the big screen
of the drive-in theatre,
beyond the inclined heads
of my sister and her boyfriend,
through the reedy voice
in the speaker
hooked onto the window,
sounding like my friend
through the tin can with string,
and the car was filled
with pungence of nearby mowed hay,
and my hand was in the popcorn,
and up there, soldiers kept
opening doors
of ovens, of showers, of dormitories,
and they were everywhere,
pale as popcorn,
and they were thrown into pits,
the bodies a nest of grubs
my friend that day had
squashed with his heel,
and my hand was in the popcorn
and that was my first taste of it.

NANCY MATTSON

Third Generation Lost Language Blues

Your blood flows
through my heart, limbs, gut
     but
     stops
at my Canadian neck
dammed at the throat

Your blood is mine
     but
     not
your tongue, lips
the language of your birth

I am guilty of collusion
in the accident of my
     unchosen
     birth
in post-war Winnipeg
condemned to a life
of English sentences

I have learned them well
their multiple undertows
pull me down
into swirling possibilities of poetry
     swyrl
from Scottish through Norse
     possibilité
from French through Latin
     poesis
from Latin through Greek

I cannot deny the delight
of tongue, ear, mind
the polyrhythmic shaping
of my Canadian heart
      but
      now

I am beginning to hear
the words that English never speaks
      suomea suruksi
      language sorrow
      laulun kieli
      language song

RHONA McADAM

Epistle

for Paul

My love writes in another language.
His large hands take the pen
on delicate journeys of curious
syllables, a sough on the tongue, a small
crashing of consonants, muted in the cave
of his mouth. He is lost
in another thinking; his large hands frame
the page, the letters
kiss across paper, silver filigree
tied into shapes that please
my love's eye, horizons of aspen
trembling words to the upper margins
of sky, the blue lines, the white
paper. I am weaving in and out of his story;
in it I speak to my love in his mother
tongue, my lips move toward him, closing
on the soft sweet song of the words
he's always meant to teach me
on winter nights like this, the cold
is a blue line of frost on which his words
hang cold as frozen birds, and his big
hands warm them into flight again
a mystery inscribed in words
I only know in dreaming, they circle
before sleep and disappear, slivers
in the blue lines, gleaming.

KIM MORRISSEY

Photograph

there is a boy leaning
down from a chair
like a pale christmas cherub
skin fluorescent in the shadow of plants

everything around him seems golden

I want to show you
the carved groove of his back
the muscle cradling his hips
the legs falling clean from his thighs

everything about him smells sweet

I remember this man in my window
bending over my plants in the nude
with his back to my camera

the air that he breathes
tastes of lemons

the water drips muddy and dark
and the holes in the pots bleed white roots
and the man

with the boy's voice
and thin shoulders
stands naked and laughs

ROGER NASH

The University of Silence

This is the curriculum of the University of Silence.
Students will provide questions for all
of the answers asked.

Why did the Byzantine Empire fail,
its bearded murals glittering wildly,
stigmata showering down golden leaf?
The speed of light remains constant through the universe.

What can prove the existence of God?
A small cloud that beats a loud tambourine.
Alternatively, but as successfully, a Smyrna fig.

Why do long-lasting marriages fail?
Yellow umbrellas may open more slowly than blue.

What, then, is love?
Two snails climb a cabbage stump.
They don't turn back. Tracks slime.

Was Socrates a Philosopher, or a husband who could think?
Red umbrellas fold as slowly as blue.

Why are there wars, still?
The speed of snails is constant through the universe.

Now unwrite your name, and lose this paper.

MICHAEL REDHILL

Caravaggio: Abraham

was only doing what his father told him.
He prepared his son for sacrifice
as if he were a cow he owned
and only an angel stopped the knife.
Isaac's life was in the hands
of a delicate mythology.

But what if that day
had turned out differently, what if
Isaac, who they say
was the perfect son, had
refused to go up, or maybe
declined his chores, or later
spurned an arranged marriage?
What if he had not laid his head down
on that rock and waited
for his father's test of faith
to be acted out on his skin?
And what if the ritual murder
had been completed, and after
Abraham still heard voices, driving him,
yet no other portents came
and he waited for a sign
as his son cooled.
Would he have then
pieced Isaac apart and devoured him
with Sarah? At that point,
what possible difference
would it have made?

This next-to-final moment is
the one you recorded, Caravaggio.
The knife is hovering
in a shaft of light that arrows
into Isaac's shouting mouth.
The angel has intervened and
a wild-eyed Abraham has not
untensed his arm, although
it is almost certain that he will.

I am thankful
for the little shaft of light
that lands on the child's mouth
in the moment of his soundless cry
for help. There is not such a great struggle
beyond Isaac's. The two forces
have already battled it out.

But that boy's mouth--that's where
you think the struggle is, don't you
Caravaggio? Not that conflict to be
the father, but to be the son,
property of the father, the
flesh commodity. Why else
is Isaac's mouth the centre
of your painting if not because
it is the soundless dark space
from where all sons emerge?

KAREN RUTTAN

Stepping into the Water

I was making dinner when I heard. Popping pearl onions from their skins, watching my husband and his father from the kitchen window as they pieced a field-stone patio with steps into the water.

Cement dished from a red wheel-barrow.

The couple next door came to tell us, calling down from the cliff as the men shifted rocks. A man up the road keeled over dead into the water while he and his sons were beaching the boat.

His wife still in town buying groceries.

I watch their mouths move, arms pointing, my husband and his dad in heavy fisherman's sweaters and garden gloves stand together, hands on hips. Interrupted, they listen and look down at their work.

She was buying groceries.

Picking over produce, selecting meat, her shopping cart full of future meals. On the drive home, how the sun must have dazzled over the car hood. The purple thistle and golden rod. Hand on the steering wheel, wedding band glittering.

The next morning, the foggy lake light. A fat, black snake rose from the rocks and fell asleep halfway up the cedar tree beside the dock. It's slick body choked around the trunk.

They were building a patio. I was making dinner. The ordinariness. What was the last thing she said to him?

Later that night, we gathered round the table playing "Trivial Pursuit," answering the big questions that earn us our wedges.

Outside, all was black, except for the light from the couple next door. They were jitterbugging; he'd swing her out the length of their arms, then coil her in close, holding her tightly for a moment, then out again.

I could not hear the music, only see her pink baby dolls spinning in the soft glow of a driftwood lamp.

Out there, was the sleeping lake. The abandoned cottage where the man died. His wife coming home, arms full of groceries. Cans of pork 'n beans rolling on the beach. The snake slipping off to a hole in the ground.

Out there, is a patio of odd-shaped field-stone, made to fit together like the pieces of a puzzle. Perfect rock slabs stepping into the water. The cracks cemented to last. The earth beginning to settle.

ALLAN SERAFINO

McArthur's Highway

At night, driving alone in his rig
McArthur is the last man on earth.

The highway is his alone, he made it
he dreams it, a silver flute slicing

through the darkness. And the wind,
that hot wind from the desert, barrels

past his open window. McArthur smells
the pine, the grease, the brassy stars.

The moon smiles down on his Desdemona,
his lovely lady. He is in love with her

throaty roar, her scandalous shimmy,
the lecherous sparkle of her body.

He has bottled up thousands of miles,
drunk lakes of hot, stale coffee

in restaurants where he can't recall any
face let alone one to remind him of home.

Won't take riders. He is the last driver.
Doesn't own a handle. Doesn't need one.

The squawk box is a dumb companion
when there's no one out there to answer

anyway. The radio honks out hurtin' songs
from Tau Ceti or stars beyond while someone,

he supposes, spins galaxies like platters,
while the pain of the vast country

squeezes his heart. He slips by
with lonesome tears, the empty cities

the mournful rivers. The great forests
hush at the sound of his passage.

In the desert's big promise he opens
Mona up and she responds like a wailin',

rollin' woman. They are heading
for the moon and the next coffee shop

this side of the Milky Way. The highway
is theirs alone. They made it. They dreamed it.

FLORENCE TREADWELL

Exiles

I have planted a perennial garden,
the mauves and blues of my childhood dresses,
the deeper violets of age.

Barbarous flower names, I hear you
spoken long before me
by my mother and grandmother
like a private language
whose echo I've carried to this new
distant earth.

This earth, I work with numb fingers,
prepare it as I do my heart
for all the partings in my life.
Roots and tendrils fasten, on the morrow
I leave.

I dreamt of this garden for years, the dormant
blues and mauves, the urgent violets—

My grandmother is dead, my mother's twisted hands
no longer move the earth: old wounds
or witchery, their voices urge my hands.
I squat, I kneel. Aching, I pry
at subterranean secrets.

Planting a perennial garden,
leaving: the same act of faith.
The same power to carry.

ANNE WALKER

Moon Big and Orange as Incandescent Light

One

Unlike intricacies of bluer and browner
          smoke
       spiralling like a C.A.T. scan in
    a blade of sunlight.

Cancer just blows up, a red safety balloon
in the front seat
of a burning car.

Two

          (afraid of stillness,
           of lying and knowing)

Three

Spider webs that hold
in this world
dissolve mechanically in surgery,

become less and less real
until to look at your body is
to understand atoms are divided by space
much bigger than matter.

Afloat underneath soft-blue
cotton blankets   you drift up from anesthetic.

Mustard colour dry on your neck.
Pulling scratch of breath coming
through chemicals, the sound of salt water
in your throat.

ANDREW WREGGITT

Singing like Crazy

We go to the river singing any old song,
you going slower and slower
in the willows and devil's club,
trail snaking down the embankment,
eyes open to shadows and the simplest
cracking of the window above us
A little nervous because of the bears
When we arrive, there are fresh tracks and droppings,
a half eaten salmon, spawner, head on the rocks,
water slipping up into its open stomach,
cool fingers saying *there, there*
Or maybe *here, here*
Don't worry I say, there is lots
to eat along this river today besides us
We stand in the water in our waders,
the river hugging our legs/knees/thighs sexual,
continuous caress and we step carefully
to avoid the full wet embrace
Feel the blunt noses of red and green salmon,
scowls and crooked snouts
bumping against our legs and we forget
about fishing for rainbows, never mind,
there is lots to eat today
besides trout
You say the river is flecked with blood
meaning red spawners holding in the shallows,
and I think of the song we are in, amazed,
ravens arguing by the back eddy,
and the deep green foliage and the bear
singing too in his silent walk and sheen
Who knows or cares who is singing?
There is only this feeling of looking at you
in the water and wonder and cool embrace of the river,
salmon touching your legs

Maybe you're right, maybe it is blood,
climbing up into the river,
up into the heart of this dry place,
into us. *Here, here*
    And we are, wet feet in the middle
of everything, laughing and still
singing like crazy

PATRICIA YOUNG

Bigger than a Bowl of Rice

*Beijing--A 17 year old Chinese girl confounded doctors when she
started to shed her skin several days after biting a python to death.*

I slithered from my mother's womb,
crescent moons glinting in my newborn
eyes, but you are not

interested in my birth, only in that day
I bathed in the river, the day I washed
my hair, then swam with my younger sisters.
They stayed to play pat-a-cake
in the mud while I fell

asleep on the bank. I dreamt
my mother had taken a lover to wash
away her grief, I dreamt her lover
was mine, that my father woke
from death and ate a meal with us.
He held my hand, touched my hair,
revealing nothing

but sadness
after all, he liked
the man. But I was angry
with my mother, at her beauty
and betrayal. What do you make
of this dream by the river?
When I woke a serpent

was licking my eyelids, its diameter
bigger than a bowl of rice.
I struggled with the python,
its unblinking eyes above me
like the eyes of my dream

lover and then I lunged
into it, biting its neck, a huge
and awful kiss. They threw

the dead snake into the Chu Kiang
and four days later my skin
began to moult from my chest
to feet. Important doctors came

from Beijing. For many months
they have hovered about me with pencils
and notebooks, raising

their eyebrows. How do I explain
this to you? How do I begin
to explain this to my mother?

Notes on the Contributors

RAFI AARON was born in Ottawa in 1959. He graduated from York University, Toronto, and for the last eight years has been residing in Israel.

BERT ALMON's sixth collection of poems, *Calling Texas*, was published recently by Thistledown Press. He teaches creative writing at the University of Alberta.

GEORGE AMABILE won the CAA medal for Literature in 1983. He has published five volumes of poetry.

BRIAN BARTLETT, a New Brunswick native who lived in Montreal from 1975 to 1990, teaches at Saint Mary's University in Halifax. His collection, *Planet Harbor*, appeared from Goose Lane Editions in 1989.

JOHN BARTON's fourth collection, *Great Men*, was published in fall, 1990, by Quarry Press. Currently living in Ottawa, he is co-editor of *ARC* and program director for the Tree Reading Series.

LAURIE BLOCK lives in Winnipeg where he is a writer and storyteller. His poems have appeared in several magazines and in the Turnstone Press chapbook, *Governing Bodies*.

WILLIAM BONNELL has had poems published in about two dozen British and Canadian magazines and anthologies. He is currently working on a collection entitled *Moving South*.

LESLEY-ANNE BOURNE was born in North Bay, Ontario. Her poems have appeared in *Grain, Event, Toronto Life*, and other journals, as well as in *More Garden Varieties* (1989).

DIANA BREBNER lives in Ottawa. Her poems have appeared in many Canadian literary magazines. Fifteen poems were included in *Distant Kin: Dutch-Canadian Stories & Poems*, Netherlandic Press, 1987.

BRIAN BRETT is the author of *Fossil Ground at Phantom Creek, Smoke Without Exit, Evolution in Every Direction, The Fungus Garden*, and forthcoming, *Alien Near the Stream*. He lives in White Rock.

JOHN BROOK was born in Shropshire in 1931, migrated to Australia in 1953, and to Canada in 1968. He was Kamloops Poet Laureate from 1986 to 1989, and has written a children's operetta, "The Poetry Tree," with Art Lewis. He is a French immersion teacher.

RON CHARACH's anthology, *The Naked Physician*, features poems about the lives of patients and doctors, by thirty-six Canadian physicians (Quarry Press, 1990).

KAREN CONNELLY lives in Calgary.

MARLENE COOKSHAW's most recent book is a collection of poems called *The Whole Elephant*. She is assistant editor of *The Malahat Review* in Victoria, B.C.

AFUA COOPER is the author of: *Breaking Chains* (Weelahs Publications, 1983); *Red Caterpillar on College Street* (Sistervision Press, 1989). Recordings: "Womantalk" (Heartbeat, 1984); "Poetry Is Not a Luxury" (Maya, 1987); and "Sunshine" (Maya, 1990). She lives in Toronto.

MICHAEL CRUMMEY was born and raised in Newfoundland, and is now a grad school drop-out living in Kingston, Ontario. His work has been previously published in *TickleAce*, *Proem Canada*, and *The Fiddlehead*.

BARRY DEMPSTER is the author of four books of poetry, most recently *The Unavoidable Man* (Quarry Press), two collections of short stories, and a children's novel. He lives in Toronto, where he is the Poetry Editor and Book Review Editor for *Poetry Canada*.

D. J. EASTWOOD is a poet living in St. John's, Newfoundland.

DEBBIE FERSHT is a graduate of the University of Toronto, Scarborough College, and spent third year at the University of Mannheim, West Germany. She has previously had poetry, prose and artwork published in *Yak*, *SCAT!* & *The Mythic Circle* (California).

ERIC FOLSOM lives in Kingston because it's the right speed. He can see shift-worker daddys and grad student moms playing with their kids.

NEILE GRAHAM is currently living in Seattle, Washington. She grew up in Victoria. Her poetry collections are *Seven Robins* (1983) and, in preparation, *Airs and Graces*.

JEFF GRIESBACH is an eighteen-year-old high school student from Toronto.

MARGARET HAMMER, of Dartmouth, Nova Scotia, has worked as a writer and a manuscript editor in New York City and Canada.

LALA HEINE-KOEHN was born in Poland and studied International Law and Voice in Munich. She emigrated to Saskatoon, Saskatchewan, where she began to paint and write; her work has been exhibited in Canada and the US. Author of four books of poetry, her work has appeared in many literary magazines and anthologies here and abroad. She lives now in Victoria, B.C.

LYNN HENRY lives in Charlottetown.

KEN HILLS was born in Toronto, has been a Brampton teacher for twenty-seven years, is a husband and father of three, as well as a novelist, short story, and poetry writer.

ALISON HOPWOOD has lived, worked, written, and published from Halifax to Vancouver. She recently published a book of poems, *As Sure As Summer* (Caitlin Press, 1989).

BILL HOWELL is writing poems again: *Antigonish Review*, *Poetry Canada Review*, *Poetry Halifax Dartmouth*, *Pottersfield Portfolio*, *Toronto Life*. The new manuscript is called *Moonlight Saving Time*.

HELEN HUMPHREYS lives and writes in Toronto. Her first book of poems was *Gods and Other Mortals*; her first novel, *Ethel on Fire*, is forthcoming from Black Moss Press.

LYDIA KWA was born in Singapore. She is near completion of a Ph.D. in Psychology at Queen's. Her work has been published in *CV2*, *Antigonish Review*, *Matrix*, and campus magazines.

VIVIAN LEWIN was born in Pennsylvania, and lives mostly in Montreal; she migrated to Florida in 1987. Her poems have appeared in *Field* and *Ariel*.

LAURA LUSH's first collection of poems will be published by Véhicule Press in 1991.

KATHY MAC currently lives, writes, and works at her day job in Halifax, N.S. She has been published in numerous periodicals and anthologies across Canada.

CAROL MALYON's first book of poetry, *Headstand*, was published by Wolsak and Wynn in 1990. A collection of short stories will appear in 1991 from The Mercury Press.

BLAINE MARCHAND's third book of poetry, *A Garden Enclosed*, will be published by Cormorant Press in 1991. He has just completed *An African Journey*, a novel based on a film.

NANCY MATTSON's *Maria Breaks Her Silence* (Coteau, 1989) was short-listed for the Gerald Lampert Award and the Writers' Guild of Alberta Poetry Award.

RHONA McADAM lives in the Canadian west.

KIM MORRISSEY's *Batoche* won third prize in the 1987 CBC Literary Competition, and was published by Coteau in 1989. His stage play, *Dora*, is about to be produced by BBC Radio.

ROGER NASH's third collection of poems, *Night Flying*, was published by Goose Lane Editions in spring, 1990. He teaches Environmental Ethics at Laurentian University.

MICHAEL REDHILL has just published his first collection of poetry, *Impromptu Feats of Balance*, with Wolsak and Wynn. He won the National Poetry Contest in 1988.

KAREN RUTTAN is a graphic artist and frequent reviewer for *Poetry Canada Review*. She lives in Toronto.

ALLAN SERAFINO has been published in numerous magazines, anthologies, and chapbooks. *Time Pieces* won prizes in *Alberta Poetry Yearbook*, *Whetstone*, *CA+B* and others. He lives in Calgary, Alberta.

FLORENCE TREADWELL was born in Bordeaux, France, and emigrated to Canada at age twenty-five. She lives in Peterborough, Ontario, where she teaches French at Trent University.

ANNE WALKER's first book of poetry, *Six Months Rent*, is coming out with Black Moss Press in spring of 1991. She is a Toronto poet.

ANDREW WREGGITT is a former winner of the CBC Literary Competition, and is the author of four books of poetry, including *Making Movies* (Thistledown Press) which won the 1989 Writers' Guild of Alberta poetry award.

PATRICIA YOUNG lives and writes in Victoria, B.C. Her most recent book, *The Mad and Beautiful Mothers* (Ragweed, 1989), won the Pat Lowther Award.